Thank you for choosing All About - books for kids.

As a family-owned independent publisher we rely on your Amazon reviews and we hope that you will share our books with your friends and family.

All About *books for kids*

Copyright © 2020 by L.E. Arning

All rights reserved. No part of this publication may be reproduced, distributed, or transmitted in any form or by any means, including photocopying, recording, or other electronic or mechanical methods, without the prior written permission of the publisher, except in the case of brief quotations embodied in critical reviews and certain other noncommercial uses permitted by copyright law.

All About Cats
All About *books for kids*

Kittens love to play, their favorite games are chasing toys and play fighting. Play fighting is how they practice their hunting skills.

Cats have extremelly good hearing, in fact, they are in the top 10 for the best hearing animals on the planet.

All kittens are born with blue eyes, some breeds keep their blue eyes but most cats have a different eye color around the time they turn one year old.

Cats sleep an average of 15 hours per day, sometime cats can sleep up to 24 hours straight.

Cats have strong backs and legs to hold them in place and help them climb trees. Their front claws are great at clinging to bark.

Cats can get allergies just like people can, they can sneeze and get runny noses.

Most cats have 30 teeth, they are very sharp but since they are pointed and not flat, cats cannot chew their food.

Cats and dogs communicate differently, the reason they often don't get along is actually just miscommunication.

Cats are usually very independent, but sometimes they do make friends with other cats.

Cats have a strong instinct to hunt for prey, they will chase nearly anything, from larger animals and humans down to bugs and even specks of dust.

Cats are very smart animals, it is likely that they are smarter than dogs, but it is difficult to know for sure because they almost always refuse to participate in tests.

Cats can be very loyal pets and research has shown that their bond to humans can be even stronger than that of dogs.

There are 15 books in the All About series

All About Alligators *ASIN: B088DCD7V3*
All About Birds *ASIN: B088DCTRJY*
All About Cats *ASIN: B087TN87L4*
All About Dogs *ASIN: B087TMHTZB*
All About Dolphins *ASIN: B088DCQBJJ*
All About Fish *ASIN: B087T2N33V*
All About Horses *ASIN: B087TQBZ9Q*
All About Kittens *ASIN: B088D9W9VY*
All About Lions *ASIN: B088DCTWTH*
All About Meerkats *ASIN: B088CMT5NP*
All About Monkeys *ASIN: B088DCFBGF*
All About Puppies *ASIN: B088DCHFQX*
All About Red Pandas *ASIN: B088D26JZC*
All About Squirrels *ASIN: B088DCT14P*
All About Wolves *ASIN: B088DD5CB6*

All About *books for kids*

Copyright © 2020 by L.E. Arning

All rights reserved. No part of this publication may be reproduced, distributed, or transmitted in any form or by any means, including photocopying, recording, or other electronic or mechanical methods, without the prior written permission of the publisher, except in the case of brief quotations embodied in critical reviews and certain other noncommercial uses permitted by copyright law.

Printed in France by Amazon
Brétigny-sur-Orge, FR